ERIN HANSON
LANDSCAPES IN OIL

Erin Hanson DESIGN

Printed in China.

Paintings and artwork bring beauty and life into your home. Art can act as a single focal point in the room, or it can be one of many cohesive elements. Either way, the choice of artwork will be an important consideration when designing your room.

Use this flipbook to inspire ideas and excite your creative juices!

White, neutral, and gray tones are the perfect backdrop for a splash of color.

Modern and traditional settings both benefit from a contemporary landscape painting.

Color blocking walls presents your painting as the center showpiece.

Here are a few examples of using blues in the home.

Yellow and gold colors are complemented with subtle beige tones.

Canvas-wrap prints can be used to decorate, as well as original oil paintngs.

Beige tones can be brought to life with a vivid oil painting.

Green and blue accents look beautiful against white and gray. Compare the effect of the color blue applied as a furniture accent (left) and as a wall color accent (right.)

Warm browns and tans work well with complementary paintings.

The color of the frame should harmonize with the furniture in the room.

Blacks and grays provide the perfect non-competing background for a colorful paintng.

Burgundy and brick tones can be brought to attention by incorporating a matching piece of artwork.

Desert-themed paintings are the perfect way to add drama to your home!

Choose fabric colors that match the painting you are hanging.

This pair of paintings creates a cohesive look in this room that would otherwise be dominated by white and brown.

Let's take a look at artwork in the workplace.

Observe how a simple splash of color livens up a reception area!

Bringing artwork into a conference room adds style and class.

Observe how paintings change their appearance on a warm wall (left) versus a cool wall (right.)

Following pages: a large diptych painting brings a panaroma of color into the home.

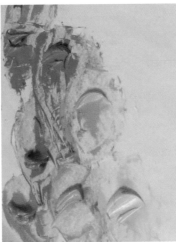

Consider commissioning an artist to create the perfect color-coordinated painting. Provide the artist with actual paint and fabric samples to make color matching a cinch.

It is never too early to consider artwork when you are building your dream home. Make sure to install spot lighting above any walls that will be showcasing your paintings.

Spot lighting comes in many different styles and colors! You can order your own fixtures online and have them installed by an electrician.

Simply choose any color present in the painting itself, and paint your entire wall in that color.

Notice the different effects you can create by using different wall colors!

A colorful painting provides endless opportunities for design!

A frame can help accentuate the painting.

Consider all the things you can do to a room to accessorize your Erin Hanson original!

Get inspired through color!

THE ERIN HANSON GALLERY

THE ERIN HANSON GALLERY
Please visit the website for
current gallery locations.

WWW.ERINHANSON.COM

Please contact us to purchase
original oil paintings, custom
prints, art books and more!

(818) 860-1623

contact@erinhanson.com